D0251093

Presented to:

_____

From:

_____

Date:

_____

Two Hearts Are Better than One

Dennis & Barbara Rainey

J. Countryman

Nashville, Tennessee

Project editor: Jenny Baumgartner

Designed by Koechel Peterson & Associates, Inc., Minneapolis, Minnesota

ISBN: 0-8499-5401-0

Printed and bound in the United States of America

www.jcountryman.com

Since 1976, Dennis and Barbara Rainey have focused their ministry on encouraging and strengthening families. They are nationally known speakers and authors. Dennis serves as executive director of FamilyLife, a division of Campus Crusade for Christ. For more information about FamilyLife conferences, "FamilyLife Today" (a nationally syndicated radio program), or other excellent resources for your family, visit them on the Web at www.familylife.com or call 1-800-FL-TODAY.

Eve speaking to Adam:

With thee conversing I forget all time,
All seasons and their change, all please alike.

John Milton
Paradise Lost

Introduction

*E*veryone has a story . . . a fascinating tale involving adventure, laughter, courage, pain, and romance.

You have such a story, and so does your mate. This book will help you share your stories, as well as write together the intriguing saga of your life together in marriage.

Think of this journal as not just a tool for better communication, but a lasting record of the growing relationship you share. We hope it will guide you to deeper transparency with each another, just as Adam and Eve were completely open and honest before the Fall. Uncovered both physically and emotionally, these original lovers shared a perfect intimate relationship.

In our fallen world, finding such transparency is a struggle. But what enjoyable "work"—sharing in the unfolding plot of a story designed uniquely by God for just the two of you!

We encourage you to take this path toward openness in your marriage. To help you begin the journey, we offer the following ideas.

Remember to Consider the Right Setting

Establish a personal, private, and special meeting place, and agree on a morning or evening sharing-time together. Some suggestions:

- Talk over a cup of hot tea or coffee at home.
- Meet somewhere for a lunch date, with plenty of time to go over a question or two.
- Get away for a weekend and talk.

What to Write

As you go through the questions, write down your answers and date them. You'll find that your answers will be important a year or many years from now.

+ Write down the words that your mate uses frequently to describe feelings.
+ Take turns writing—the husband recording his wife's responses and vice versa.
+ Write down additional questions that come to mind during your time together. (We've included a few pages at the back of this book to list them.)

Remember to Listen

Listen, and look each other in the eye as you share and talk together.

+ Listen . . . and seek above all else to understand your mate.
+ Listen . . . and rephrase your mate's answers when appropriate.
+ Listen . . . and don't retreat when it feels uncomfortable. Share what's really important.
+ Listen . . . and try not to defend yourself. Remember, "winning" is not the goal; understanding is.
+ Listen . . . and don't react negatively to your mate's answers. Instead, encourage each other to share deeper feelings by asking more questions.

Now turn the page and begin another great adventure in your life—discovering and authoring the book of your love.

Dennis and Barbara Rainey

If you could keep only one memory
(of some past event or period of time),
what would it be? Why?

His Response:
_____
_____
_____
_____
_____
_____
_____
_____
_____
_____
_____
_____
_____
_____
_____
_____
_____
_____
_____
_____
_____
_____
_____

Her Response:

What are the five most important
milestones we've passed together?
Why was each so important to you?

His Response:

_____

_____

_____

_____

_____

_____

_____

_____

_____

_____

_____

_____

_____

_____

_____

_____

_____

_____

_____

Her Response:

In what single way would you most like to see me grow personally in the next twelve months?

His Response:

_____
_____
_____
_____
_____
_____
_____
_____
_____
_____
_____
_____
_____
_____
_____
_____
_____
_____
_____
_____
_____
_____
_____

Her Response:

_____
_____
_____
_____
_____
_____
_____
_____
_____
_____
_____
_____
_____
_____
_____
_____
_____
_____
_____
_____
_____
_____
_____
_____
_____
_____

Who are your three closest personal friends?
What do you enjoy most about each one?

His Response:

Her Response:

What do you think have been the most romantic times we've had together? How can we keep the romantic side of our marriage alive and exciting?

His Response: _____

_____

_____

_____

_____

_____

_____

_____

_____

_____

_____

_____

_____

_____

_____

_____

_____

_____

_____

_____

_____

Her Response:

What two or three problems, if solved,
would make the most positive difference
in our marriage and family?

His Response:

Her Response:
_____
_____
_____
_____
_____
_____
_____
_____
_____
_____
_____
_____
_____
_____
_____
_____
_____
_____
_____
_____
_____
_____
_____
_____

What do you see as the three most important decisions we need to make this year? Toward what choices are you leaning in each area? What would help us make each decision wisely?

His Response:

_____
_____
_____
_____
_____
_____
_____
_____
_____
_____
_____
_____
_____
_____
_____
_____
_____
_____
_____
_____

Her Response:

_____

_____

_____

_____

_____

_____

_____

_____

_____

_____

_____

_____

_____

_____

_____

_____

_____

_____

_____

How would you describe your ideal day
(sunup to sundown)? Your ideal evening?
Your ideal weekend?

His Response:

Her Response:

If you could spend one uninterrupted hour today with any person alive, who would it be? (It can be anyone!) What would you do or discuss? Why?

His Response:

Her Response:

I prize thy love more than whole mines of g

If ever two we

If ever two were one, then surely we.

If ever man were loved by wife, then thee;

If ever wife was happy in a man,

Compare with me, ye women, if you can.

I prize thy love more than whole mines of gold,

Or all the riches that the East doth hold.

My love is such that rivers cannot quench,

Nor ought but love from thee give recompense.

Thy love is such I can no way repay;

The heavens reward thee manifold, I pray.

Then while we live in love, let's so persevere

That when we live no more we may live ever.

Anne Bradstreet

In what three specific ways could we improve our everyday communication? Where are we strong in our communication? Where do we hit snags?

His Response: _____

_____

_____

_____

_____

_____

_____

_____

_____

_____

_____

_____

_____

_____

_____

_____

_____

_____

_____

_____

_____

_____

_____

_____

_____

_____

Her Response:

If you knew you had just six more
months to live, how would you spend them?
What would you do? Where would you go?

His Response:

_____
_____
_____
_____
_____
_____
_____
_____
_____
_____
_____
_____
_____
_____
_____
_____
_____
_____
_____
_____

Her Response:

What are the three biggest needs in the world
. . . the kinds of things about which you say to
yourself, "Something must be done about this"?

His Response:
_____
_____
_____
_____
_____
_____
_____
_____
_____
_____
_____
_____
_____
_____
_____
_____
_____
_____
_____
_____
_____
_____
_____

Her Response:
_____
_____
_____
_____
_____
_____
_____
_____
_____
_____
_____
_____
_____
_____
_____
_____
_____
_____
_____
_____
_____
_____
_____
_____

Which work or home responsibilities
do you find most fulfilling? Which
do you find most frustrating?

His Response:

_____

_____

_____

_____

_____

_____

_____

_____

_____

_____

_____

_____

_____

_____

_____

_____

_____

_____

_____

Her Response:

In your opinion, what three things
produce the most stress in your life?
How can I help you overcome them?

His Response:
_____
_____
_____
_____
_____
_____
_____
_____
_____
_____
_____
_____
_____
_____
_____
_____
_____
_____
_____
_____
_____

Her Response:

Of all of the gifts you've received, which do you cherish most? Of all the gifts you've given, which did you enjoy giving the most?

His Response:

_____

_____

_____

_____

_____

_____

_____

_____

_____

_____

_____

_____

_____

_____

_____

_____

_____

_____

_____

_____

_____

_____

_____

Her Response:

Have you ever received a compliment that was particularly meaningful to you? If so, who said it? How did it affect you? Have you ever given a compliment that really touched someone else?

His Response:

Her Response:

What pops into your mind when you think of
your best meal? Your best day ever? Your best job?

His Response:

_____

_____

_____

_____

_____

_____

_____

_____

_____

_____

_____

_____

_____

_____

_____

_____

_____

_____

_____

Her Response:

What is your fondest childhood memory?
Who was your favorite relative when you
were a child? What was your favorite toy?
Your favorite holiday?

His Response:

_____
_____
_____
_____
_____
_____
_____
_____
_____
_____
_____
_____
_____
_____
_____
_____
_____
_____
_____
_____

Her Response:
_____
_____
_____
_____
_____
_____
_____
_____
_____
_____
_____
_____
_____
_____
_____
_____
_____
_____
_____
_____
_____
_____
_____
_____

What dreams have you followed? What dreams
have you thrown away (or kept secret)?

His Response:

Her Response:

How do I love thee? Let me count the ways.

I love thee to the depth and breadth and height

My soul can reach, when feeling out of sight

For the ends of Being and ideal Grace,

I love thee to the level of every day's

quiet need, by sun and candlelight.

I love thee freely, as men strive for Right;

I love thee purely, as they turn from Praise,

I love thee with a passion put to use

In my old griefs, and with my childhood's faith.

I love thee with a love I seemed to lose

With my lost saints,——I love thee with the breath,

Smiles, tears, of all my life!——and, if God choose,

I shall but love thee better after death.

Elizabeth Barrett Browning

I love thee freely

I love thee purely

I love thee with a passion

do I love thee?

If you could do anything in the world
(and be certain of success), what would you do?

His Response:

Her Response:

_____
_____
_____
_____
_____
_____
_____
_____
_____
_____
_____
_____
_____
_____
_____
_____
_____
_____
_____
_____
_____
_____
_____
_____

What struggles are weighing on you?
Is there any way I can help? How can
I make your life easier or better?

His Response:

_____

_____

_____

_____

_____

_____

_____

_____

_____

_____

_____

_____

_____

_____

_____

_____

_____

_____

_____

_____

Her Response:

What do you think are my
three greatest strengths? How do they
complement your strengths?

His Response:

_____

_____

_____

_____

_____

_____

_____

_____

_____

_____

_____

_____

_____

_____

_____

_____

_____

_____

_____

Her Response:

_____

_____

_____

_____

_____

_____

_____

_____

_____

_____

_____

_____

_____

_____

_____

_____

_____

_____

_____

_____

Describe your most embarrassing moment.
Also, share your most touching experience.

His Response:

_____

_____

_____

_____

_____

_____

_____

_____

_____

_____

_____

_____

_____

_____

_____

_____

_____

_____

_____

_____

_____

_____

Her Response:

_____
_____
_____
_____
_____
_____
_____
_____
_____
_____
_____
_____
_____
_____
_____
_____
_____
_____
_____
_____
_____
_____
_____
_____

If you were suddenly removed from me by something unexpected (such as death), from what people would you most want me to seek comfort and help? Whose counsel would you most want me to avoid? Why in each case?

His Response:

Her Response:

What do you consider the three
most important things we could do with
each of our children in the next year?

His Response:

Her Response:

If we became richer than either of us could imagine today, what would you like to do with the money?

His Response:

Her Response:

What three things produce the
most stress in our marriage and our family?
How can we overcome them?

His Response:

_____

_____

_____

_____

_____

_____

_____

_____

_____

_____

_____

_____

_____

_____

_____

_____

_____

_____

_____

Her Response:

In what single area do you most
want to grow personally in the next year?
Why? How can I help you?

His Response:

_____

_____

_____

_____

_____

_____

_____

_____

_____

_____

_____

_____

_____

_____

_____

_____

_____

_____

_____

Her Response:

Rough winds do shake the darling b...

Shall I compare thee to a summer's day?

Thou art more lovely and more temperate:

Rough winds do shake the darling buds of May,

And summer's lease hath all too short a date:

Sometime too hot the eye of heaven shines,

And often is his gold complexion dimmed,

And every fair from fair sometime declines,

By chance or nature's changing course untrimmed;

But thy eternal summer shall not fade

Nor lose possession of that fair thou owest,

Nor shall Death brag thou wander'st in his shade,

When in eternal lines to time thou growest:

So long as men can breathe or eyes can see,

So long lives this, and this gives life to thee.

William Shakespeare

If we were stranded alone on an island for one month, what topic would you most like to discuss? Besides necessities of food, clothing, and shelter, what would you most want to have with you?

His Response:

Her Response:

_____

_____

_____

_____

_____

_____

_____

_____

_____

_____

_____

_____

_____

_____

_____

_____

_____

_____

_____

_____

Of all the people you've known in your life,
which three do you admire most? Why?

His Response:

Her Response:

If our house caught on fire
(and everyone was safely out), what three things
would you most want to save? Why?

His Response:

Her Response:

Why do you think we are still happily married when many people around us are not? What are the essential elements of a healthy relationship?

His Response:

Her Response:
_____
_____
_____
_____
_____
_____
_____
_____
_____
_____
_____
_____
_____
_____
_____
_____
_____
_____
_____
_____
_____
_____
_____
_____

What do you enjoy most about our sex life?
How can I improve? What do you wish
I would or wouldn't do?

His Response:

_____

_____

_____

_____

_____

_____

_____

_____

_____

_____

_____

_____

_____

_____

_____

_____

_____

_____

_____

_____

Her Response:

_____
_____
_____
_____
_____
_____
_____
_____
_____
_____
_____
_____
_____
_____
_____
_____
_____
_____
_____
_____
_____
_____
_____
_____
_____

When you pray, how do you imagine God?
How do you imagine heaven?

His Response:

Her Response:

_____
_____
_____
_____
_____
_____
_____
_____
_____
_____
_____
_____
_____
_____
_____
_____
_____
_____
_____
_____
_____

Describe what you want your life to be like in retirement. What do you want our life together to be like at that time? What steps should we take today to get there?

His Response:

_____
_____
_____
_____
_____
_____
_____
_____
_____
_____
_____
_____
_____
_____
_____
_____
_____
_____
_____
_____

Her Response:

Tell about someone who
influenced your life profoundly. How did that
person do it? What is the most meaningful
piece of advice you've ever received?

His Response:

Her Response:

In what ways do I cherish and encourage you?
How can I do better?

His Response:

_____

_____

_____

_____

_____

_____

_____

_____

_____

_____

_____

_____

_____

_____

_____

_____

_____

_____

_____

_____

_____

_____

Her Response:

_____
_____
_____
_____
_____
_____
_____
_____
_____
_____
_____
_____
_____
_____
_____
_____
_____
_____
_____
_____
_____
_____
_____

What is your favorite book or song?
How has it touched you?

His Response:

_____

_____

_____

_____

_____

_____

_____

_____

_____

_____

_____

_____

_____

_____

_____

_____

_____

_____

_____

_____

_____

_____

_____

Her Response:

_____
_____
_____
_____
_____
_____
_____
_____
_____
_____
_____
_____
_____
_____
_____
_____
_____
_____
_____
_____
_____
_____
_____

Love suffers long and is kind;
love does not envy; love does not
parade itself, is not puffed up;
does not behave rudely, does
not seek its own, is not
provoked, thinks no evil;
does not rejoice in iniquity,
but rejoices in the truth;
bears all things, believes all
things, hopes all things, endures
all things. Love never fails.

I Corinthians 13:4-8

Love never fails.

What holiday do you enjoy most?
What do you like to do during that time?

His Response:

_____
_____
_____
_____
_____
_____
_____
_____
_____
_____
_____
_____
_____
_____
_____
_____
_____
_____
_____
_____
_____
_____
_____
_____
_____
_____

Her Response:

What new tradition would you like to
start in the family? Why? What was your
favorite tradition growing up?

His Response:

_____

_____

_____

_____

_____

_____

_____

_____

_____

_____

_____

_____

_____

_____

_____

_____

_____

Her Response:
_____

_____

_____

_____

_____

_____

_____

_____

_____

_____

_____

_____

_____

_____

_____

_____

_____

_____

_____

_____

_____

What are your spiritual strengths?
How would you like to grow spiritually?
What can I do to encourage you in this area?

His Response:

_____

_____

_____

_____

_____

_____

_____

_____

_____

_____

_____

_____

_____

_____

_____

_____

_____

_____

_____

_____

_____

_____

Her Response:

What would you still
like to learn to do? Why?

His Response:

_____

_____

_____

_____

_____

_____

_____

_____

_____

_____

_____

_____

_____

_____

_____

_____

_____

_____

_____

_____

_____

_____

_____

Her Response:

What is the most enjoyable time we've ever had together? What is the saddest time? What is the one experience you hope we'll still have together?

His Response:

_____

_____

_____

_____

_____

_____

_____

_____

_____

_____

_____

_____

_____

_____

_____

_____

_____

_____

_____

_____

_____

_____

_____

Her Response:

What would you want said about
you at your funeral? What would you like
people to remember about you?

His Response:

_____
_____
_____
_____
_____
_____
_____
_____
_____
_____
_____
_____
_____
_____
_____
_____
_____
_____
_____
_____
_____
_____
_____

Her Response:

Describe the most interesting person
you ever met. What were the qualities that
made that individual so outstanding?

His Response:
_____
_____
_____
_____
_____
_____
_____
_____
_____
_____
_____
_____
_____
_____
_____
_____
_____
_____
_____
_____
_____

Her Response:

Where would you still like us to go?

What would you like to do once we got there?

His Response: _____

_____

_____

_____

_____

_____

_____

_____

_____

_____

_____

_____

_____

_____

_____

_____

_____

_____

_____

_____

_____

_____

_____

_____

_____

_____

Her Response:

What stands out most to you about
the first time we met? Our first date?
Our first year of marriage?

His Response:

_____

_____

_____

_____

_____

_____

_____

_____

_____

_____

_____

_____

_____

_____

_____

_____

_____

_____

_____

_____

_____

_____

Her Response:

_____
_____
_____
_____
_____
_____
_____
_____
_____
_____
_____
_____
_____
_____
_____
_____
_____
_____
_____
_____
_____
_____
_____

the love which

O Perfect Love, all human thought transcending,
Lowly we kneel in prayer before your throne,
That theirs may be the love which knows no ending,
Whom you forevermore unite in one.

Perfect Life, be now their full assurance
Of tender charity and steadfast faith,
Of patient hope and quiet, brave endurance,
With childlike trust that fears no pain or death.

Grant them the joy which brightens earthly sorrow;
Grant them the peace which calms all earthly strife,
And to life's day the glorious unknown morrow
That dawns upon eternal love and life.

Dorothy F. Gurney

What do you remember most about
our wedding? Do you remember how you felt when
you woke up that day? Who were the people you
talked to before the ceremony?

His Response:

_____

_____

_____

_____

_____

_____

_____

_____

_____

_____

_____

_____

_____

_____

_____

_____

_____

Her Response:

What is your view of the Bible's influence in our lives? What Bible verse puzzles you the most? Which blesses you the most?

His Response:

Her Response:

What are the three most important
values we want to teach our children
before they reach adulthood?

His Response:
_____
_____
_____
_____
_____
_____
_____
_____
_____
_____
_____
_____
_____
_____
_____
_____
_____
_____
_____
_____
_____

Her Response:

What are the times of quiet you value most?
What feelings do you experience when you are quiet?
Does God speak to you in your silence?

His Response:

_____
_____
_____
_____
_____
_____
_____
_____
_____
_____
_____
_____
_____
_____
_____
_____
_____
_____
_____
_____
_____
_____
_____
_____
_____

Her Response:

What is your favorite leisure activity or hobby?
When and where did you start doing it?
Why do you enjoy it?

His Response:

Her Response:

_____
_____
_____
_____
_____
_____
_____
_____
_____
_____
_____
_____
_____
_____
_____
_____
_____
_____
_____
_____
_____
_____
_____
_____

Growing up in your house,
in what room did you feel most comfortable?
Why? What did you do there?

His Response:

_____

_____

_____

_____

_____

_____

_____

_____

_____

_____

_____

_____

_____

_____

_____

_____

_____

_____

_____

_____

_____

_____

_____

Her Response:

Our questions:

His Response:

Her Response:

Our questions:

His Response:

_____

_____

_____

_____

_____

_____

_____

_____

_____

_____

_____

_____

_____

_____

_____

_____

_____

_____

_____

_____

_____

_____

_____

_____

_____

_____

_____